Add Value to Every Sale: Using This Technique Could Double Your Profit

Category: Business & Economics

Author: Bob Oros

Publisher: Bob Oros Publishing

ISBN: 978-1-387-19900-6

Copyright 2017

Description: It takes practice to use this technique but the dividends are great. By applying this technique you will learn how to buy everything you buy for less. Using this as a sales person you will be able to sell everything for more. Just as you play poker to win, not just to make the other players like you, this will make you a winner.

Key words: food service sales, sales coaching, sales techniques, motivating sales people, job in sales, sales manager training, sales course, manufacturing sales training, wholesale sales training, online sales training, distributor sales training, food sales jobs,

ISBN 978-1-387-19900-6

1. How to add value to every product you sell.

A sales rep recently told me a great story about how to keep from giving a discount or from having to negotiate the price. He was having the brakes adjusted on his car and the cost was $140. When he asked, "Is that the best you can do" here is how he responded: "If you want to negotiate the price – the break job will cost you $150!"

Think about what a great answer that is. What is he really saying? He is saying that I am already giving you the best price I can. He is saying that if you want to negotiate I will raise the price to $150 and we can see if you can get me down to the bottom price of $140.

Try it. If someone asks if that is the best you can offer, quote a higher price and say that is the price for folks who want to negotiate. Or say that is what everyone else is paying and you have already cut the price.

That brings up a good question: Is it part of a customer's job to ask you for a discount? Should you ask for a discount when you buy something? My answer to both questions is absolutely yes! If the sales person didn't ask the mechanic for a discount he would never have learned that great strategy.

I am reluctant with everything I buy and you should be too. The only reason I let go of a dollar bill is to get a better grip on it. I work hard for my money and I want to stretch it as far as I can. So do you and so do your customers? I want to get every ounce of value out of every dollar I spend.

It takes practice to be a reluctant buyer but the dividends are great. By being a reluctant buyer you will learn how to buy everything you buy for less. By being a reluctant seller you will be able to sell everything you sell for more. Just as you play poker to win, not just to make the other players like you.

Your price is based on a lot of factors and making a profit is not optional. You have to get paid. When you study the reactions of people who are trying to sell something to you, a reluctant buyer, you will learn the best strategies as well as see them in action.

It takes GUTS to ask for things and the more you do it the better you are at it. You might be called a few names in the process, but so what.

This reluctance should also be used when you are selling something and asked to lower your price. NEVER GIVE IN TOO EASILY! Never lower your price without setting up several roadblocks, speed bumps and detours. Let's say I have a car for sale in my driveway with a $1500 sign. You pull in. I immediately go out to the car and take the price down. I have a new sign that says $2500. I explain that I didn't realize the prices were so high and the car dealership would give me so much for my trade-in. I tell you that I will let the car go for $1500 if you try it out and like it and buy it now. But if you come back tomorrow the price will be $2500. You buy it at $1500, the price I wanted to sell it to you for.   You might think that's a little cruel. You can tell that to the person standing next to you in the unemployment line. Or you can get a job at the post office where the price of a stamp is the price you pay! (Sorry, you can probably tell I had to learn all this the hard way).

By lowering your price reluctantly you are actually adding value to your product or service. If you lower your price too easily you will actually CHEAT THE BUYER out of the good feeling they get when they know they got you to come down.

I was sitting on the plane and the woman sitting next to me was in advertising sales. When I asked her what her biggest mistake she ever made in sales, here is what she told me. "I was calling on a pawn shop with my sales manager. He told me the bottom line price for the advertising program was $1,500, but to try to get $2,000 and go down slowly and reluctantly so you "add value" to the program. When the customer asked for the price I made a huge mistake and said $1,500! The customer ended up paying $1,400 and I ended up getting chewed out!"

Here is another reason you should be slightly reluctant when giving a price reduction. An accountant once told me that I should forget the term "gross profit" and replace it with "contribution to overhead." He said that every time I lower the price I am giving part of the company away! The warehouse cost is .04%, the sales department cost is .04%, the transportation department is another .04%, administration cost is .04% and the bottom line should be at least .04%. When you cut your price below .20% think about what part of the company you are cutting out and giving away! Which vacation day would you like to give up? How much do you want you insurance deductible to go up? Which customer service person would they like to tell that they can't buy shoes for their kids this week, etc?

You don't want to appear too hungry for the sale or too eager to give everything away. The buyer will be suspicious and begin to wonder why you are so anxious to make a sale.

When you do have to lower your price never come down in equal increments. If you do you will set up a pattern. The customer will know that to get a discount all they have to do is follow your "pattern" and get a lower price.

If someone asks for a discount, after you've presented your services and quoted a price then you say: "Sure, I can for $400 but that would be without the _____ and the _____." You actually eliminate things so that they understand that as the price shrinks so does value.

Another good response when asked to discount your price is to use the "fork in the road" response. Our company came to a "fork in the road" and had to decide if we were going to be simply a price seller or if we were going to be a value seller. We chose to be a value seller and the customers we serve know that in the long run, the value of our high quality products along with our service and support, is like an insurance policy that helps them become successful.

It is necessary to discount your price from time to time. However, you deserve to get paid. Ask your customer if they have any employees who work without being paid. What kind of quality would you expect them to produce? What level of customer service would you expect them to provide to your customers? How much do you think they would end up stealing from you over time?

If your customer's business is down and they are trying to "cut their way into profitability" they are doomed to fail. The only way to increase business and get more customers is by doing it the old fashioned way. By selling!

~~~~~~~~~~~~~~~~~~~~~~~~~

"Just today, I called and placed an order for Direct TV. The salesman went through the whole speal and at the end said I need to give him $300 today. I said thank you, but no thank you because I knew he was full of crap. Then he said hold on, let me think, then he magically gave it to me for $19.00. I knew before I ever made the call that this is how the call would turn out. Had I of charged the $300, he would have laughed all day at my stupidity. I said that to say this, it's all a game. Sure some people may feel good after having bargained you down to a fair price, but others would not. I didn't feel any better, I just felt like he was insulting my intelligence."
Kimberly Burgess

"I am such a penny pincher it would be hard for me to give a discount. I always want to get my monies worth. I am willing to give a "Small" discount to make them feel good about getting us to go down on our price some. I usually can talk them into paying our price because we do deliver what we promise. I know every company has a budget but I have one too. I believe if we have a successful meeting we can come to terms to where I am not losing money and they will think they are getting something for nothing. You have to have your mind set on how far you are willing to drop your price and make sure it is worth it. You must be willing to come to each other terms. They have their mind set just like you have yours. It is like I said they will try to get something for nothing. "

Nina Hall

"Bob, this is one of the lessons from your in person course that I am now using every day. "Is that the best you can do?" I use that daily as a consumer. My husband finds it embarrassing but he likes the fact that many people will actually give you a better deal. On the flip side, when a customer asks me a price, I am no longer lowering my price. I keep it at regular cost and if the customer repeats the cost, I act surprised. I have added several dollars to my bottom line in just the month since I have returned from

your training."
Candy Swift

"I have started using this approach more and more with my customers and for the most part it seems to work however you do get those 1 or 2 customers that don't fall for it and say never mind I don't need it. But what I have found out is that the next week that they ask about the same product to see where my price is at, I would usually take it up about .20 and would you believe it they take it. They realize that they better get it now because the price seems to be going up and should have taken up on it the previous week. Live and learn and I say."
Sarah Jones

"Very good information. I'm in the process of looking for a car right now and I think this will come in very handy for me. I need a car so badly that I was willing to just take what I could get, but now I feel armed with a good bit of valuable information. I will try this tactic when I sit down at the table with the sales person. I'll let you know how it goes."
Brian Spraggins

"Being reluctant to give a discount makes the buyer feel like he has won the battle after the sale has been made. Also, if the buyer is happy then he will most likely turn into a repeat customer. When someone asks for a discount and a number pops in your head to take off the original proposal, split that figure in half or even thirds and see where it leads. Example: Seeing certain figures on paper or anywhere for that matter is all a head game. Which looks better…$4,000.00 or $3,900.00? Just by reducing the price by $100.00 can make it look much more appealing to a buyer. "

David Bradley

"A day late and a dollar short! I needed this lesson two weeks ago. I am normally fairly good with negotiations; this one client wanted to go straight to the bottom line, which I did. NOTE TO SELF: Don't give out your bottom line number!!!! I gave him the bottom line number and 2 days later he came back with a lower price. They were adamant on not paying what we bottom lined. Moral of the story- I lost $$$. Ouch- expensive lesson. Been there, done that and it won't happen again."

Teresa Cloninger

"Automatically reducing your fee is making a statement that you are not confident in your own ability to deliver a good/better product or service to the potential customer. I feel it says that a person does not value their own self worth. I'm a firm believer if I going to work hard to deliver an excellent service that I should be compensated for my effort and diligence in providing that service. On numerous occasions I have encountered sales people that just give it away without a fight, resulting in loosing money not only for the company, but themselves. The number #1 reasoning I hear is "we have to lower our prices because our competitors are" My thinking is if the customer is taking the time to discuss their needs with you, then the competitors they are currently working with at a lower rate must not be doing something right, otherwise the customer wouldn't be talking with other vendors. Sale people should not focus on "all" the reasons why they need to reduce their fee, but concentrate on all the reasons why they "shouldn't" reduce their fee.

Carla McCrea

2. How to make yourself more trustworthy and believable.

I was recently in Toledo and a sales person told me about a friend of his who sells parachutes! He said CUSTOMERS ASK FOR A DISCOUNT!

I always encourage sales people to ask for a discount when buying something to see how the person reacts to your request.   However, there are a few exceptions. In certain cases you might want to pay a little extra. For example, open heart surgery. Or perhaps a root canal. And of course it would be a good idea to give an extra tip to the person packing your parachute! In these cases you might even want to take it a step further. You might want to have them give you some PROOF OF THEIR PROMISED RESULTS.

One of the big mistakes sales people and marketers make is exaggerating rather than offering PROOF of the promised results. When you are selling an idea or trying to convince someone of something, you may be tempted to over exaggerate your claims. To get your idea across you may feel you have to use such overworked phrases such as:

"We are number one..."

"We are the best in the business..."

"You can save big money with us..."

As soon as one of these statements is made a red flag goes up in the customer's mind. In your opening statement you have just "unsold" yourself. The buyer, customer or person you are trying to convince knows immediately that you are stretching the truth. The customer always has three questions that have to be answered:

1. "So what?"

2. "What's in it for me?"

3. "Can you prove it?"

Instead of using the above overworked phrases you should use facts, figures, and examples in your presentation or sales letter to justify your statements. These facts make the buyer willing to accept you and your offer. Your goal is to weave the facts into the conversation that makes the buyer understand the LEGITIMACY of what you are saying.

For example, I recently set up a local business with an email system and the results were instant. The company had only 98 email addresses, however, I was able put together a campaign and within 24 hours 52 people opened the email, 25 clicked through, and 10 customers purchased services totaling nearly one thousand dollars. This was business that would have been lost if it were not for the promotion. Needless to say the company is now eagerly collecting the email addresses of their customers.

Like a shrewd attorney, you want to present your facts in the strongest possible light as we did in the above example.

Here are a few more:

"For example our program will increase your profits as much as 6% - here is how."

"For example this product line will cut your labor cost as much as 3% - I have the facts right here to prove what I am saying."

"For example this new marketing system will increase your sales by at least 5% - let me show you what I mean"

An idea is sold not necessarily when you go into your close, but when the customer agrees with your statements - and that is what you are looking for - customer commitment.

The truth is that a customer does not care about you or your program. They are interested in the things that benefit them - nothing else.

It is always to your advantage to support your presentation with backup evidence from impartial sources. Expert testimony is hard to challenge. Having back up information by a third party is a high standard of legitimacy that will win their confidence.

Precedent is the single most powerful legitimization - precedent is reasoning from a prior sale or situation. Lawyers use precedent judgments to prior similar cases when they make an argument.

What examples can you find in comparable situations that resemble the presentation you are making? The more examples you can find to support your case, the better.

Give examples of actions taken by other customers in similar circumstances. For example: "XYZ Company put the product in and within two month's added $5,000 in additional sales" or "Mary tried this idea in her department and was able to increase output by 23%".

Customers have a natural skepticism about most people trying to sell them something or presenting a new idea. This skepticism is something you should be aware of and prepared to overcome. This skepticism is also a powerful tool YOU can use for undermining the power of the facts or figures someone is presenting to you.

When you are presenting your price and are then presented with a competitor's price that seems much too low, you might use skepticism to your favor. You do this not by debating the accuracy, but rather questioning the source of the price. Without challenging the accuracy or correctness of the customer's position, ask how the price was arrived at.

For example, if the customer quotes a low price - ask where they got the number. Do not object - just inquire as to its rationale. Whenever a statement of fact is made, or a lower price put on the table, or an assumption is put forward as though it were obvious or non-controversial, let YOUR warning bell signal you and ask yourself "Says who?"

~~~~~~~~~~~~~~~~~~~~~~~~

"When you exaggerate, initially you've blown the whole meeting. As soon as you make an exaggerated comment your potential customer is going to doubt the rest of what you say. They do not care if you are the best or number one that does absolutely nothing for them. Be legitimate with your statements. Whatever statement you make you should be able to prove it if needed."

Matthew Thacker

"Exaggeration can come back to bite you. If you are being legitimate, you should look the buyer in the eye and do not look away. People read with their eyes and might not think you are sincere if you are not looking straight at them. Ask some of your customers if you might be able to use them as a reference when presenting a product to a new buyer, this should help them see that you are being legitimate about the facts of your product."

Jordan de la Morandiere

3. Stop buyers when they are shocked at your price.

Not long ago I attended a two day seminar designed for buyers. The seminar was about teaching these professional purchasing managers how to be better negotiators. The instructor started off with an example about how a company implemented just ONE negotiating strategy for one year to see what effect it would have on the company's profit. After the year was over the company was able to show an improvement of one million dollars strictly from this one concept.

They had a more glamorous name for this powerful strategy; I simply call it price shock! And it is one of my best techniques to use as well as to talk about.

The best story I have ever heard about price shock is from a buyer who claimed he could get a sales person to lower their price without saying a word. He said he was able to perfect his "price shock" strategy by practicing on his way to work every morning.

What exactly is "price shock?" It is a simple facial expression that says, "Your price seems high!" Well-trained buyers are taught to use this strategy with exact precision.

When a buyer is looking at your initial price they are taught to wrinkle their forehead as if to say "you are much higher than I expected!" This is designed to immediately put you, the presenter, on the defensive. The sad part is it works most of the time. Even if you have a close relationship with the buyer, you may misread it as a sign that you should lower your price to get, or keep, the business.

Work on your own price shock until you can perfect it. Every time you buy something act surprised at the price. Watch closely how the seller reacts. If you are buying a new house, tell the realtor you are shocked by the price. When you are in the market for a new car, try it on the car sales person. When you buy a new TV, tell the clerk you are shocked at how much the price is.

To become an expert at how effective price shock is you should practice your own unique style for acting surprised every time a price in presented to you. Whenever you are given a price on anything, act slightly surprised – watch carefully how they respond. Simply say "the price is a little high", or "I am sure this is a nice hotel, however, your price seems a little high", or "I was thinking about buying a new boat, however, your price seems a little high!"

For example, a large horse trailer dealership in Dallas was setting up a meeting for all their sales and management people and needed to book a large block of hotel rooms. This was right after they attended my seminar and they decided to give it a try. He called me and said the results were amazing. The savings was $2500. Not bad for a little theatrics.

Do I use this strategy – absolutely – I use it every time I am presented with a price! I stay in many hotels during the course of a year. Does price shock save me money? One hundred hotel rooms x $10 average savings = $1,000 per year!

When I check in I ask for the price – act slightly shocked – pull out my deck of discount cards – act shocked at the discount price and many times get a lower price than the lowest discount.

What about when someone is shocked at YOUR PRICE? What should your reaction be? There are four responses you can use to counter this powerful strategy:

1. You can be weak, give in, and lower your price. They won. This is what most buyers expect, especially from an amateur sales person.

2. You can be shocked at their shock. This is designed to neutralize the strategy. The customer is shocked at your

price; you are shocked at their shock. Seems a little strange to use at first, until you see how well it works. This throws the shock right back at the buyer and you have now put the buyer on the defensive. Then stay silent. Do not provide an explanation. It is the buyer's turn to make the next move! This is so effective you will have a hard time keeping a straight face. Role play this and get it down to a science.

3. You can use the "Feel, Felt, Found" reply. Here is how it works: "I understand why you feel that way, everyone I talked to so far today felt the same way, until they found out that the market has gone up since last week."

4. You can justify your price rather that discount it. This is an extension of number three. "I understand why you might feel that way, everyone I talked to today felt the same way, until they found out what is included in that price." And then begin to list the additional benefits that are included, which makes the price seem smaller and smaller.

5. There is a response called a "fork in the road" response that sometimes works on price shock:

"Our company came to a fork in the road and had to make a choice on whether to be a low cost, no service, no frills type of company, or to be one that provides services, follow up, and extra benefits. We chose the latter. One other thing to consider Mr. Prospect, you get me. I go with the deal - and if you don't think I can make a difference - try me."

Bottom line - There are plenty of folks who want to buy just on price and the sales people who sell them could be replaced with a fax machine.

~~~~~~~~~~~~~~~~~~~~~~~

"Whenever possible, don't discuss price until you've discussed the validity of your pricing. If forced to give a price prematurely, only offer a range. Ask questions that will help you understand what the client wants. Always add 10 to 20 percent to your high end. It's a lot easier to go back with a lower price than a higher one. If the customer is going to choke on your artificially high price, he'll choke on your real top end price, and you'll lose the advantage of being able to quote a final price that is lower than he expected.
Yessie Narvaez

"I try to avoid the "Shock" effect altogether. I believe in managing expectations up front. 1st I find out if they have used a similar service in the past; if not I walk them through the process and briefly mention the cost (giving a wide range). This should prepare the person for negotiations. If they try to use the "Shock" effect – don't flinch. Counter with the "Triangular negotiation" method. Here you are negotiating three different variables; if you change one side- I change another side. So no matter what type of triangle you end up with (right, acute, obtuse, equilateral, isosceles or scalene) its still a TRIANGLE. A win-win-win for every one."

Teresa Cloninger

"I never thought of reacting to shock with shock---I always thought I had to explain why or "attempt to get a lower price". It works though...I tried it by simply saying "REALLY!!" with a bit of shock on my face and said nothing else....He bought the product and we moved on like nothing happened."

Ken Jones

"I actually used the shocked approach yesterday when it was tried on me - IT WORKED! I said that the previous person had the same shock when they saw the price of the meat slicer, but when I explained that I came along with the deal for service, and explained how the unit would assist with profitability, and that I helped them save a lot by directing them to the unit they need to fit their needs... they found that the price was great, and purchased immediately.

We got to the 'fork in the road' moment, where I thought I might lose the sale, and went silent. They were a little thrown off, and about ten long seconds later, they asked for the slicer to be boxed up, and asked if I could assist them in finding the rest of the wish list they were carrying. That was a big sale, and an especially happy customer."

Craig Young

"Price shock immediately gives you a sense of guilt, which you have to learn to overcome right away and be ready with a come back. A lot of buyers are shocked at the price because they do not understand the quality of the product such as a home use item compared to a commercial item. Our job is to convince the buyer that it is the right product for their needs and a good value for their money."

Jordan de la Morandiere

4. When you are unable to talk to the decision maker.

A good lesson learned a while back was from a sales person in Twin Falls, Idaho. A friend of his sold a service station to someone from another country that didn't understand how we do business. The new owner would order a part from the auto supply store and then try to negotiate the price with the driver.

You may be thinking how anyone could do something that dumb. However, if we go into a customer's business and are not talking to the decision maker, we are doing the same thing.

Another perfect example of this strategy in action was demonstrated while checking into a hotel in North Platte, Nebraska. I asked the clerk at the front desk for a discount. She said she had to check with the manager and went back into the office. When she returned she said she was sorry but the manager said that was the best they could do. I walked over to the elevator and while waiting another person came in and asked for a discount. The clerk did the same thing only this time I could see the entire office. It was empty. She simply walked into the office, stood there for about five seconds and returned.

Sometimes a decision maker will use a "higher authority" to hide the fact that they are the decision maker. For example: "This agreement looks good, but I will have to run it by my committee (or wife or any other higher authority)."

Using the higher authority is when the customer or prospect does not have responsibility for making the buying decision. It is usually a "buying committee" that has the final say.

The next time you buy a house or car watch carefully how the sales person will remove this roadblock. The sales person will say, "If we find the house (or car) that you really like, is there any reason you could not make the purchase today?" Once they get the green light, the sales person will spend whatever time it takes to find you the right product. If you say your husband or wife has to give the final approval, the sales person will try and set up an appointment when both of you can be present.

To avoid being the victim of the higher authority, be sure all parties necessary to make an agreement when you are making your presentation. For example, if one of the buyers is not present, it is best to postpone the meeting until everyone can be there. If one of the critical parties is not there, that person can veto everything that was agreed upon.

If you are the one making the presentation and the presence of someone important is impossible, set a short one or two day time limit for his or her higher authority approval.

You can use this same strategy. You can start your presentation with the same question. "If I show you a program that will not only save you money on your operating expenses, but also lower your labor cost as well as increase your sales, is there any reason why you would not want to give it the go-ahead?" If the buyer has to get approval from a higher authority you will know how to tailor your presentation.

If you are making a presentation to a person who does not have authority to make the decision, the best strategy is to build up the person you are presenting. Suggest to the person that the committee is surely influenced by what he or she says. If you can get them to commit to making a "sale" to the committee, it can be embarrassing if he or she is not able to get it through for you.

Another strategy if you are selling to a buyer who has to "run it by the committee" is to ask about the possibility of making a presentation to the committee yourself. This can either call their bluff or it may present you with an opportunity to actually make a presentation to the buying committee.

When making YOUR presentation it is to your advantage to present a higher authority from which you must get approval. Even if you do have complete authority over the selling price, you may want the buyer to believe you have to get approval.

If both buyer and seller could say to the other, 'I know what I am doing and I have the power to make the best deal possible' it seems as though the selling process would be much easier. This is not always the case. When you have the authority to make the final decision the buyer knows that he or she only has to convince you and does not have to work quite as hard if you are the final authority. Once you have given your okay, the sale is done.

Not so with the person who has to answer to a higher authority. When you have to have approval from your department manager, sales manager, purchasing manager, marketing manager, or even the president of the company, then the customer must do much more than convince you, he or she must present a reason you can take to your higher authority for approval.

This is only a tool you should be aware of and use when the situation calls for it. There are many times that it is not necessary and you can be the final authority without any problem.

"Every salesperson should know how important it is to have the key players in the room before you pitch your product or service. The logic behind this is that whoever you pitch to is going to go to the decision maker and try explaining what you told them and who knows what there going to say or how they are going to make your product or service look. Nobody should know your product or service better that yourself, so don't you think you need to be the one selling it and not some schmo sent there just to make you think your doing your job!"

"A good question I learned a long time ago is "Other than "_____", is there any other reason we can't do business today. If its Price, Other than the price, is there any other reason we can't do business today? This is a great question to ask to find out exactly what you need to fix or

change, to make the sale today!"
David Bradley

Unfortunately for high dollar services there is a Higher Authority or Two or Three…….The best case scenario to ask about making your presentation to everyone at once. I don't seem to live in that magical little world. Sometimes you have to overcome the objections one at a time- one level at a time. One thing I have found helpful as you get buy in at each level; ask what objections you think the next level will have. This helps you be a little more prepared and the more buy in you have the better. Hey, if life was easy- what fun would it be?
Teresa Cloninger

I think this is a very interesting concept. I have often used this, without having truly thought about it and the process. One thing I do realize from this lesson is that, by offering to make your presentation to the committee or decision maker, it takes some of the pressure off of the non-decision maker. I have seen relief in a front office person's face, when I asked to speak directly with the decision maker. Not only have you gotten to the person you really need to speak to, you have also forged a more comfortable relationship with the person who can get you there.

Tonya Sauer

There are many uses of the higher authority strategy and you should understand how it works so that you can respond effectively when they are used against you. One of the most common uses is to obtain a delay without directly asking for one. In this way, the absent authority provides an opportunity for the salesperson to go back, think through the positions of each side, and evaluate the proposed agreement. It works for me!

Yessie Narvaez

I knew a guy that owned a communications company and had vice president as his title on his business card. Even though he owned the company, he always had an "out" to use the higher authority whether he was selling his product or someone was making a presentation to him. It is definitely a good idea to build up the person who is not the decision maker. Making them feel they are part of the process for a major decision is great way to get them on your side.

Gregg Nixon

Many times I might say to an individual "I know you don't want to hear all of this twice. Is there anyone else who will need to hear my information today?" You would be surprised how many times the prospect will say "Let me see if Joe is busy" or "Maybe Sherrie can meet with us, too. I also might say "This is a lot to remember. Would you like anyone else present so you don't have to ………

Lynn Mosely

5. Make it difficult for the customer to ask for a discount.

Good guy/bad guy is taking the higher authority strategy to the next level. The good guy/bad guy can be obvious or it can be quite subtle. It can be carefully planned in advance, or people can fall into the roles naturally.

When this buying strategy is used, you might not even notice until you have become the victim. The real estate agent and client often use this method. For example, the home seller might play the bad guy, holding out for top dollar. But the seller's agent plays the good guy by showing the bad guy why the price is above market value.

Husband and wife teams often use this method too. The husband is usually the bad guy while the wife is more reasonable and sympathetic to the other side's viewpoint.

Good guy/bad guy occurs when there are two or more buyers and one is easier to get along with, provides more information, or seems more anxious to make a deal, while the other is more difficult.

I recently sold a travel trailer and was amazed at how most husbands and wives fall into these roles. The wife would make the initial call and get all the information before handing the phone over to the husband, the bad guy, to talk about the price.

We have all seen the good guy/bad guy tactics on television. A suspect is caught and interrogated. The first detective puts him under a glaring light, hits him with hard questions and roughs him up.

The tough guy leaves. In comes the nice guy who gives the suspect a cigarette and lets him relax. Soon the suspect spills all he knows.

Car dealerships are known for this. When the sales person says "I will take this to the sales manager and see if I can get this price for you", they actually make us believe they are on our side!

Here is how it works in a car dealership. Let us assume you and the salesperson have reached a price agreement. The salesperson has to get "approval" from the manager "Bad Guy" to honor his/her agreement with you. However, only the sales manager can accept an offer. The salesperson is a messenger between you and the sales manager.

The next time this is strategy is used on you - try this: tell the sales person that you want to go into the sales manager's office together - you want to see how the sales person is going to work for you to get the price you want. They will tell you that is not possible - insist on it.

You can do the same thing when a buyer insists on a lower price. You can call your manager (the bad guy) and report back that the manager was really tough on you, "However, I was able to get the price down a small amount. Not quite what you want, but pretty close." This makes the customer believe you are on their side.

When faced with the "good guy/bad guy" routine do not fall for it! The buyers both have the same goal - to get you to give everything you have.

Another heavy-handed but effective tactic of intimidation is to out-number the other party. You show up alone; the buyer brings in the lawyer, the accountant, the executive vice-president, and so on.

If you think your opponent is using Good Guy/Bad Guy, do one of two things. Let the other side know you have recognized the tactic, or bring in a Bad Guy of your own.

Good Guy/ Bad Guy is a very effective way of putting pressure on people, without confrontation. Counter it by identifying it, people use this tactic on you much more than you might believe. Don't be concerned that the other side knows what you are doing. In fact, when you are negotiating with someone that understands all of the gambits, it becomes more fun!

Yessie Narvaez

Actually, depending on the good guy/bad guy routine, you can work it to your advantage. For example, I bought a brand new car 2 years ago. I took my brother in law in with me to use his discount (since he's an employee of that car manufacturer). The sales person used the whole bad guy/good guy routine. Payments worked out to 5 years at X dollars per month - but only came with a selected warranty. That was the best price he could give me.

The next day, I go in, sign the papers, and then I'm waiting for the sales person to bring my new purchase around. I was walking around the dealership - and right into the sales manager's office by mistake. I talked to him for a few minutes and told him that I was surprised myself that I bought another car from that manufacturer, considering I had been lied to by the sales person when I bought the car prior to that one (same manufacturer). I went out, and grabbed stuff from my old car.

Before I left the dealership, the sales person called me in - the sales manager came up with a new deal. Payments were then a little lower than X dollars per month, for 4 years, and with a bigger warranty package! The point is to recognize it, and work it to your advantage!

JoAnne Welch

I hate playing games- I don't like the Good Guy / Bad Guy routine. There is nothing wrong with negotiations; but the bottom line is the bottom line. Sometimes it is better to walk away from business. Not all sales are good. YES you heard me right- sometimes it better to turn down the business. If the customer is playing games now- what will they do in the future? Can they be trusted? Ask a few probing questions and see if the buyer really has to get approval from the "higher authority". IF not and they are just playing games; ask them to give you a call when they grow up. Just say it nicely!!!! Truth in Sales,

Teresa Cloninger

Most car repair shops think that when a woman comes in she dose not know anything about cars. Well, I have replaced many things on a car or truck from a fan belt, water pumps, engine gaskets, and all the way down to the UV joints. I don't claim to be a pro but I do now how to do these things and understand some car repairs are harder than others. I usually get my own parts and then call the different shops to see who has the best price on installation. Some still try to quote me prices that are too high in my opinion, and if they do I bring in my husband to play the part of the bad guy.

Laura Arnett

6. A seven word phrase that will make you a ton of money.

This seven-word strategy has the power to save you thousands of dollars each year. If you use this seven-word question seven times you will save money. I use this strategy every chance I get.

Here is an example. I had a meeting in San Jose, California and when I called to reserve a room the price was $289 for one night.

My reply was $289 FOR ONE NIGHT? I live in Oklahoma, that's a month's rent, including utilities! The lowest I could get them down to was $269.

Instead of taking the room I decided to drive around looking for something a little less expensive. I came across a name brand hotel and asked the clerk how much a room was for the night. The woman behind the counter said $189. I decided to use the "is that the best you can do" question - also called "the squeeze" - and see if I could get a discount.

My first tactic was to use price shock. She came down to $169. Next I asked her if that was the best she could do. She came down to $149. Then I asked her if she had any specials going on and she lowered the price to $99. I asked her one more time if she could do any better explaining that I was on a tight budget and anything over $100 (including taxes) would cause me a lot of problems.

She lowered the price to $89!

TWO HUNDRED DOLLARS less than what the first price I was given when I first came to town! There are several things she could have done to get a higher price.

First, she came down too easy and too fast. If she had been slightly reluctant I would have stopped asking for a lower price.

Second, she could have said it was obvious that you have not checked the price at the Hilton - I would have stopped asking for the lower price.

Third, she could have said she had to check with the manager (higher authority) and walked in the back room for a moment - returning, she could have said the manager would not let her go any lower (even if the manager was not in the office).

Fourth, when I was shocked at her price, she could have acted surprised at my shock. This would have stopped me by making me feel slightly embarrassed - well, maybe a normal person would have been embarrassed.

This seven-word statement has saved me an untold amount of money over the years.

I was recently in Los Angeles working with a group of sales people and the "is that the best you can do strategy" was thoroughly explained. One of the sales people called me the next day and said he was able to save TWO THOUSAND DOLLARS on a software program he was buying.

I was working with a group of sales people in Las Vegas and a sales person called me the next day and said he was able to save EIGHT HUNDRED DOLLARS on a landscape project he was purchasing for his new home.

I was in Allentown Pennsylvania and one of the managers called me the next day and said he was able to save FIVE THOUSAND DOLLARS on a contract he was working on.

What should you do when someone asks you if that is the best you can do?

First, simply say yes.

Second, if they insist on a lower price you can consult with your "higher authority."

Third, if they still insist you can turn your higher authority into a "bad guy".

Fourth, if they still insist on a better price and you feel that to give in a little will guarantee the sale, you might come down on your price a very small amount and act as if you are really going out on a limb and taking a chance (reluctance).

~~~~~~~~~~~~~~~~~~~

I really enjoyed the training in Richmond. I used "is that the best you can do" on the airline after I missed my connection flight back to Sarasota. I was given a free hotel, dinner, breakfast and $100.00 off my next flight. So yes it does really work.

Timothy Emmett

I am going to do a little experiment this weekend. At EVERY garage sale I attend, I will ask "Is that the best you can do?" - Even if it is on something that costs $.50. I can't wait to see how much money I can save on items that I'd usually pay the sticker price for! Morgan, my co-worker is coming with me, so I will have a witness to be sure that I follow through with my plan. Once I see it in action, I will definitely be compelled to use this when making bigger purchases. When someone poses this question to me, surprisingly, the word "Yes" does wonders. People have the same thought that I do…"At least I asked."

Laura J. Czajka

I have used all four tactics, depending on the situation. The reluctance tactic is most popular. I tried (is that the best you can do) the other day. I do know if I was getting a great deal, but I asked anyway. The salesperson (owner) simply said yes, and I could not get them to go lower. I did feel a little guilty, but not as much would have been in the past - so I am making progress.

Jordan de la Morandiere

I love this concept. After reading this I gave it a try. I made a reservation at a hotel. They told me the cost would be 119.00 for a king room. I ask, "Is that the best you can do?" He then told me he could give me a two doubles for 109.00. I replied, I have stayed at your hotel in the past and will more than likely stay again, but not at those prices. Long story short, I paid 75.00, for the king. I am so excited that this worked so easily I can't wait to use it again.

Tonya Sauer

I like this response because I think we forget to ask this of our vendors that we work with on a daily basis in our offices. To our equipment company, 'is that the best you can do?' to our office supply company, 'is that the best you can do?' to our t-shirt supply person, 'is that the best you can do?' We must be prepared to respond to our clients as well when they ask the same of us. All of things our cost covers should be in our response to this question. 'Why yes, Mr. Customer, that is the best we can do based on the following: Fica, Futa, Suta, Workers Comp, administrative fees, recruiting fees, qualifying fees, background and drug testing...etc.'. We too are in this business to make money, so yes that is the best we can do.

Kristan Wilson

7. How to overcome every objection.

Abraham Lincoln had a reputation as a lawyer for hardly ever losing a case. His strategy was to unknowingly use the feel/felt/found formula to perfection, however, he probably never heard of it.

Lincoln would never argue or attack an opponent. In fact, Lincoln, at first, would argue his opponent's case telling all the reasons why his opponent was right. He'd appear to agree to all the things his opponent said.

As his opponent was stating his case before the jury Lincoln would write down everything that was said. Then he would begin changing the minds of the jurors by saying, "We all feel these things are true, and my opponent has skillfully presented them in a way that anyone hearing them would have felt the same, however, there are a few other things that influence this case and when I present them you will find that the way to vote will be obvious."

Then he'd begin slowly with his own arguments. He was a master at diplomacy, at getting people to change their minds and feel good doing it.

Lincoln probably invented the "feel/felt/found formula even though he never heard of it. The feel/felt/found formula can become one of your most valuable tools. Try this response when you get a negative reaction to the price you are presenting or the program you are trying to push through.

"I can certainly understand why you feel the price seems a little high".

"I don't blame you for wanting to get the best value for your money and at the same time keeping your cost down to a minimum."

"Every person I talk to has felt the same as you do when they first looked at the program".

However, after they found out that the small difference in price for the higher quality product was actually the best investment they ever made they saw it from a completely different view."

Practice this a few times and people will never know why they are all of sudden agreeing with you.

I understand how you FEEL...

Everyone I talked to today FELT the same...

Until they FOUND out that the market has gone up!

~~~~~~~~~~~~~~~~~~~

I can see where this tactic could be beneficial in some situations but not every. It all depends on the client you are pitching too. Also, the product or service that you're selling is a factor. Once you get to the point where you say, "know why you feel this way", you have already gotten them worked up or mad or put on the defensive side. Then if you come back with, "everybody else felt the same way," well they are going to wonder why the heck you still trying to sell something that gets everybody all worked up. Maybe you should see a pattern of previous clients getting defensive about what you are selling and try something new. Basically, I am saying make it sound irresistible and pitch it right the first time, close the deal and move on to the next potential client!

David Bradley

Nothing takes the wind out of someone's sails faster than when you use this strategy! When you start with an agreement it befuddles them. I remember once during a debate in college when I used this approach- my opponent spattered and sputtered "you can't agree!!!" I continued on using facts that turned that agreement around. I won. Our minds are always racing- the buyer is already coming up with the next answer to what they THINK your objection to their objection is going to be. (You know when they get that smug look on their face.) Sometimes you have to short circuit the opponent's brain to get them to stop and listen to you. This is one approach that definitely works.

Teresa Cloninger

The great thing about this tactic is that gives you extra time to change people's mind when necessary. Sometimes, something will come up in a negotiation that you were not expecting. You have not heard anything like this before. It shocks you. You do not know what to say; but if you have Feel, Felt, Found in the back of your mind, you can say, I understand exactly how you feel about that. Many other people have felt exactly the same way. However, by the time you get there you will have recovered your composure and will know exactly what to say.

Yessie Narvaez

This is a grand strategy. It also explains a lot about this dynamic individual. Having the ability to turn the tables on your client without them realizing it would be a great skill to develop and the neatest part about the plan is that you are not being dishonest with them in any way, you are simply starting from the side they are most likely already on and allowing them to convert to your beliefs on their own terms. This is a lesson I would like to learn and implement.

Kathie Luttrell

About the author Bob Oros

Regardless of whether you are reading one of his books or attending one of his programs, the most frequent comment is: "This guy has been there, he is one of us, I am going to use these strategies."

With over 2,000 speaking engagements in all 50 states and several international locations for manufacturers, distributors and associations, you can be sure you will get the results and information you are looking for. Prior to starting his speaking career, Bob served six years in the US Navy as a Communications Specialist and then worked his way from a street sales person to the position of National Sales Manager for a Fortune 200 company.

Bob has received awards for speaking, writing and marketing too numerous to mention.

Additional Topics by Bob Oros

Why Sales People Fail

The Key to Selling Anybody

Add Value to Every Product

Never Make the First Offer

How to Justify Your Price

Lost in 60 Seconds

One Good Reason to Buy

Control a Buyer's Attitude

How to Create Demand

Smoke Screen Objections

Take the Risk Out of Sales

How Small Companies Get Big

www.ingramcontent.com/pod-product-compliance
Lightning Source LLC
Chambersburg PA
CBHW021925170526
45157CB00005B/2189